Quick and Easy
Stir-fries

Pat Chapman

Contents

Published exclusively for J Sainsbury plc
Stamford House Stamford Street
London SE1 9LL
by Martin Books
Simon & Schuster Consumer Group
Grafton House 64 Maids Causeway
Cambridge CB5 8DD

Published 1997
ISBN 0 85941 952 5
© 1997 Martin Books

Printed and bound in Italy
Design: Moore Lowenhoff
Photography: Jean Cazals
Styling: Antonia Gaunt
Food preparation: Oona van den Berg
Typesetting: Cambridge Photosetting Services
Pictured on the front cover: Pork with Cashew and Sweet and Sour Sauce, (page 8)

Introduction
I guess we all think of Chinese wok dishes as the definitive stir-fries. And it is true that, with their crisp textures, fresh flavours and bright colours, they are fine examples of the art of stir-frying, but they are by no means the only examples. I have taken the liberty of delving far and wide into the world's culinary 'stir-fry' larder to select the recipes for this book. I hope you'll agree that the range of tastes and styles is very wide, and, in some cases, unexpected.

I have not omitted Chinese dishes; indeed as you would expect, they come first. Following them are their near-relatives, stir-fry dishes from Thailand. Less well known are Indian stir-fries. I have adapted popular favourites, such as korma and tikka masala, to the rapid stir-fry method. Equally excellent is my selection of stir-fries from Mexico, America, the Mediterranean, and northern Europe, many of them adaptations of other cooking methods. I have selected as wide a variety of ingredients as possible. Stir-fries benefit from really fresh ingredients.

Stir-frying is a very spontaneous way of cooking: you can, if you wish, buy the ingredients you need to make a particular recipe, or you can open the fridge, see what there is to use up, and then find a recipe to fit what you have. You can choose one theme for your meal, such as Indian, or you can mix dishes from different countries to create a truly international menu. With stir-fries there are no rules.

In some of these recipes I have used minced garlic, ginger, basil etc. These products are available bottled – which helps make your stir-fry particularly quick and easy – but you can, of course, substitute fresh herbs and spices if you wish.

RECIPE NOTES
All recipes in this book give ingredients in both metric (g, ml, etc.) and imperial (oz, pints, etc.) measures. Use either set of quantities, but not a mixture of both, in any one recipe.

All teaspoons and tablespoons are level, unless otherwise stated.
1 teaspoon = a 5 ml spoon;
1 tablespoon = a 15 ml spoon.
Egg size is medium, unless otherwise stated.
Fruits are medium-size, unless otherwise stated.

PREPARATION AND COOKING TIMES
Preparation and cooking times are included at the head of the recipes as a general guide; preparation times, especially, are approximate and timings are usually rounded to the nearest 5 minutes.

Preparation times include the time taken to prepare ingredients in the list, but not to make any 'basic' recipes.

The cooking times given at the heads of the recipes denote cooking periods when the dish can be left largely unattended, e.g. baking, and not the total amount of cooking time for the recipe. Always read and follow the timings given for the steps of the recipe in the method.

Chinese Stir-fries

Until the revolution pronounced them decadent, China had more restaurants and tea houses than anywhere else on earth. A few decades ago, Peking had over 45,000. In our favourite Chinese restaurants, huge jet-black woks are held over whooshing yellow flames, while their glistening contents are deftly tossed by master chefs. There's nothing like it for pure theatre. And there's nothing easier to do at home – perhaps without the whooshing and tossing – but with equally mouth-watering results. Here are eight favourites from the Chinese restaurant.

Chicken Chop Suey

Preparation time: 5 minutes + 15 minutes cooking.
Freezing: recommended. Serves 4.

Chop Suey means 'chopped mixed food'. In other words, you can include any suitable ingredient; here the star ingredient is chicken.

300 g (10 oz) boneless, skinless chicken
   breast
2 tablespoons sunflower oil
2 or 3 garlic cloves, sliced
2.5 cm (1-inch) cube of ginger, peeled and
   sliced finely
100 ml (3½ fl oz) chicken stock

4–6 spring onions, chopped
300 g packet of fresh mixed stir-fry vegetables
3 tablespoons sherry (any type)
2 teaspoons chilli sauce (optional)
1 teaspoon soy sauce
salt

❶ Cut the chicken into 2 cm (¾-inch) cubes.

❷ In a wok, heat the oil until it is quite hot. Add the garlic and ginger and stir-fry for about 30 seconds. Add the chicken and stir-fry briskly for about 4 minutes.

❸ Add the stock. Simmer and stir for about 3 more minutes.

❹ Add the onion and mixed vegetables, sherry, chilli sauce (if using) and soy sauce. Continue to stir-fry for about 2–3 minutes more.

❺ Check that the chicken is cooked by cutting a piece in half. It should be white all the way through. If not, continue stir-frying until it is. Season with salt.

Veal with Broccoli and Rice Noodles

Preparation time: 30 minutes + 20 minutes cooking.
Freezing: recommended. Serves 4.

This is an attractive dish with an interesting colour contrast.

250 g (8 oz) dried rice stick noodles

625 g (1¼ lb) lean veal steak, partially frozen

3 tablespoons soya or sunflower oil

2 or 3 teaspoons minced garlic

1 teaspoon minced ginger

250 g (8 oz) broccoli florets

6 spring onions, chopped

1 green pepper, chopped

light soy sauce, to taste

salt and freshly ground black pepper

❶ Soak the noodles in ample cold water for 20–30 minutes. Put them into boiling water for 5 minutes or until they are tender. Drain and set aside.

❷ Cut the meat into thin strips, ideally about 5 cm (2 inches) × 2.5 cm (1 inch) × 5 mm (¼ inch). It is easier to cut the meat thinly if it is still almost frozen.

❸ Heat the oil in a wok until quite hot. Add the garlic and the ginger and stir-fry for about 30 seconds.

❹ Add the meat and stir-fry briskly for about 8 minutes, turning the meat frequently to prevent the meat from

sticking; gradually lower the heat, and add splashes of water as necessary. Add the drained noodles, and gently, so as not to break them, stir-fry them until they are well mixed in.

❺ Boil, microwave or steam the broccoli until it is tender.

❻ Add the broccoli, onion and green pepper, and continue to stir-fry for the least possible time – just enough to ensure the meat is cooked right through (at least 4 minutes). Add some soy sauce to taste, season with salt and serve.

Pork with Cashew and Sweet and Sour Sauce

Preparation time: 5 minutes + 15 minutes cooking.
Freezing: recommended. Serves 4.

Pork is China's favourite meat. The notion of mixing sweet syrupy tastes with savoury ones and then adding a slight tartness (with lemon juice) originated in Canton.

625 g (1¼ lb) lean pork steak, partially frozen

3 tablespoons sesame oil

4 tablespoons raw unsalted cashew nuts

1 tablespoon sesame seeds

2 or 3 tablespoons minced garlic

1 teaspoon minced ginger

6 spring onions, chopped

1 red pepper, de-seeded and chopped

1 carrot, shredded

125 ml (4 fl oz) sweet and sour sauce

1 tablespoon chilli and garlic sauce

1 tablespoon tomato ketchup

1 teaspoon light soy sauce

lemon wedges

salt

❶ Cut the meat into thin strips, ideally about 5 cm (2 inches) × 2.5 cm (1 inch) × 5 mm (¼ inch). It is easier to cut meat thinly if it is still almost frozen.

❷ Heat the oil in a wok until it is quite hot. Add the cashew nuts, sesame seeds, garlic and ginger. Stir-fry for about 30 seconds.

❸ Add the meat and stir-fry briskly for about 8 minutes, making sure the meat

gets turned frequently; lower the heat gradually to prevent the meat sticking and add splashes of water if necessary.

❹ Add the remaining ingredients, except the lemon wedges and salt, and continue to stir-fry for the least possible time – just enough to ensure the meat is cooked right through (at least 4 minutes). Season with salt, squeeze over some lemon juice, then serve.

Chinese Fried Rice

Preparation and cooking time: 10 minutes.
Freezing: recommended. Serves 4.

1 tablespoon sunflower oil

2 or 3 spring onions, chopped

50 g (2 oz) diced mixed vegetables, thawed if
frozen

50 g (2 oz) straw mushrooms, halved

450 g (15 oz) cooked rice

1 teaspoon dark soy sauce

salt

❶ In a wok, heat the oil until it is quite hot. Add the onions and stir-fry for about 2 minutes.

❷ Add the vegetables and mushrooms, and when hot, add the rice.

❸ Briskly, but gently (so as not to break up the rice), stir-fry everything until it is hot.

❹ Add the soya sauce and season with salt.

Black Bean and Green Pepper Duck

Preparation time: 5 minutes + 15 minutes cooking.
Freezing: recommended. Serves 4.

Duck is as popular as chicken in Chinese cooking. This classic combination uses green pepper for colour and a sauce made from the black soya bean for a delicious flavour.

425 g (14 oz) boneless, skinless duck breast

2 tablespoons sunflower oil

2 teaspoons minced garlic

1 teaspoon minced ginger

125 g (4 oz) black bean sauce

1 green pepper, de-seeded and chopped

1 green chilli, de-seeded and sliced (optional)

4–6 spring onions, chopped

dark soy sauce or salt

❶ Cut the duck into 2 cm (¾-inch) cubes.

❷ In a wok, heat the oil until quite hot. Add the garlic and ginger and stir-fry for about 30 seconds. Add the duck pieces and stir-fry briskly for about 5 minutes.

❸ Add the black bean sauce. Simmer and stir for about 3 more minutes.

❹ Add the pepper, chilli and onion. Continue to stir-fry for 2–3 minutes more.

❺ Check that the duck is cooked all the way through by cutting a piece in half. It should be the same colour throughout. If it isn't, continue stir-frying for a little longer.

❻ Add soy sauce or salt to taste.

Tofu and Chinese Vegetables

**Preparation time: 5 minutes + 10 minutes cooking.
Freezing: not recommended. Serves 4.**

Tofu is a kind of cheese made from soya beans – yet another
fascinating Chinese invention.

200 g (7 oz) fresh tofu

50 g (2 oz) mange tout or snow peas, halved

350 g packet of fresh mixed oriental stir-fry
   vegetables

2 tablespoons sesame oil

2 teaspoons minced garlic

2 teaspoons minced ginger

4–6 spring onions, chopped

1 tablespoon red pepper, de-seeded and
   chopped

100 g (3½ oz) fresh beansprouts

soy sauce

salt

red chilli, shredded, to garnish

❶ Slice the tofu into 8 mm (⅜-inch) squares.

❷ Drain the mixed vegetables, reserving the liquid and chop the vegetables into bite-size pieces.

❸ In a wok, heat the oil until it is quite hot. Add the garlic and the ginger and stir-fry for about 30 seconds. Add the onion and red pepper and continue to stir-fry for 2 or 3 minutes more.

❹ Add the mange tout or snow peas, the mixed vegetables and beansprouts, and cook them until they sizzle. Then gradually add the vegetable liquid over the span of a couple of minutes, maintaining a sizzle so that the liquid thickens slightly.

❺ Add the tofu and stir gently to prevent it breaking up. Continue stir-frying until the tofu is hot.

❻ Season with salt and soy sauce. Garnish with shredded red chilli and serve.

Fish with Lemon Sauce and Noodles (Chow Mein)

Preparation time: 5 minutes + 15 minutes cooking.
Freezing: recommended. Serves 4.

The Chinese invented the noodle. It is as important a staple to them as rice. Chow Mein means 'stir-fry noodles'. Here noodles are made with a delectable fish and tangy lemon sauce.

2 tablespoons sunflower oil

2 teaspoons minced garlic

1 teaspoon minced ginger

4–6 spring onions

2 or 3 tablespoons chopped orange or yellow pepper

2 tablespoons Chinese lemon sauce

100 ml (3½ fl oz) fish or vegetable stock, or water

250 g (8 oz) boneless cod steaks, cut into bite-size pieces

125 g (4 oz) instant egg noodles

3 tablespoons sweet sherry

soy sauce

salt

To garnish:

1 tablespoon flaked almonds

1 tablespoon snipped chives

❶ Heat the oil in a wok until it is quite hot. Add the garlic and ginger and stir-fry for about 30 seconds. Add the onions and pepper and continue to stir-fry for 2 or 3 minutes more.

❷ Add the lemon sauce and the stock. When it is simmering, add the fish.

❸ Simmer for 6–8 minutes.

❹ Cook the noodles: bring a saucepan of water to the boil and immerse the noodles. Bring the water back to the boil. Turn off the heat. Put on the lid and leave the noodles for 5 or 6 minutes. Drain.

❺ Add the hot noodles very carefully, stirring them into the wok ingredients.

❻ When everything is hot, add the sherry and season with salt and soy sauce. Garnish with the almonds and chives and serve.

Chinese Prawn Curry

Preparation time: 5 minutes + 15 minutes cooking.
Freezing: recommended. Serves 4.

The Chinese restaurant curry is quite unlike its Indian or Thai counterpart. Here the orange juice cuts through the richness of the sauce. Serve with rice and other Chinese dishes.

2 teaspoons mild or medium curry powder

1 tablespoon cornflour

4 tablespoons soya or sunflower oil

2 teaspoons minced garlic

4–6 spring onions, chopped

450 g (15 oz) peeled, cooked prawns

100 g (3½ oz) canned sliced bamboo shoots

2 teaspoons fresh orange juice

1 teaspoon sugar

1 tablespoon tomato ketchup

salt and freshly ground black pepper

❶ Mix the curry powder and cornflour with 2 tablespoons of oil and 1½ tablespoons of water to make a smooth runny paste with the consistency of cream.

❷ Heat this paste in a non-stick saucepan, stirring continuously to prevent it from going lumpy. When it starts to thicken, add a little more water. Keep stirring. When it starts to thicken again, add a little more water. Repeat this process until it will not thicken further; you are aiming for a thickish, pourable sauce. Keep warm.

❸ Heat the remaining oil in a wok. Stir-fry the garlic and onions for a couple of minutes. Add the prawns and the bamboo shoots, and stir-fry briskly until they are hot right through.

❹ Add the warm curry sauce, orange juice, sugar and tomato ketchup. Stir-fry until sizzling and hot. Season with salt and pepper and serve.

Thai Stir-fries

Until the 90s Thai food was little known in Britain, and tended to be dismissed as a cross between Indian and Chinese. It has been influenced by these cuisines but, as these recipes show, it is quite distinct from both of them. I have included the famous dish, satay, and two Thai curries, and one curry-flavoured rice, but they are unlike any Indian curry. There is a noodle dish which would be Chinese if it were not for the fabulous aromatics of Thai flavourings. I have also included Thailand's most popular soup, Tom Yum, which starts out as a stir-fry, and is irresistible. And I could not resist including an aromatic salad which is stir-fried first and then chilled.

As for flavours and aromas, think lemon grass, lime leaves, coriander, garlic, chilli and basil and you are on the Thai track. Fortunately all the Thai ingredients you need are now readily available at Sainsbury's, and once you have them, the cooking is quick and easy and the results really tasty.

Tom Yum Stir-fry Soup

Preparation time: 5 minutes + 20 minutes cooking.
Freezing: recommended. Serves 2.

This is Thailand's most famous soup. It starts out as a stir-fry, and stays in the wok to become a delicious soup.

2 tablespoons sunflower oil

1 teaspoon Thai red curry paste

2 teaspoons minced garlic

2 lemon grass stalks, fresh or bottled, chopped finely

2 or 3 lime leaves, fresh or dried

2–3 spring onions, chopped

½ tablespoon chopped red pepper

½ tablespoon chopped green pepper

1 or 2 whole red chillies, de-seeded and chopped finely

400 ml (14 fl oz) chicken or fish stock

50 g (2 oz) chicken breast stir-fry fillets, cut into small, thin strips

50 g (2 oz) small raw, shelled prawns

3 tablespoons finely chopped basil

salt

❶ In a wok, heat the oil until it is quite hot. Add the curry paste and garlic, and stir-fry for about 30 seconds.

❷ Add the lemon grass, lime leaves, onions, peppers and chillies and 3 or 4 tablespoons of the stock. Stir for about 3 more minutes.

❸ Add the chicken strips and the prawns.

Continue to stir-fry for 2 or 3 minutes more.

❹ Add the remaining stock and simmer for about 8 minutes, stirring from time to time.

❺ Add the basil and season with salt. Simmer for a couple of minutes more and serve.

Beef or Lamb Penang Thai Curry

Preparation time: 10 minutes + 15 minutes cooking. Freezing: recommended. Serves 4.

This typically aromatic Thai curry originates from neighbouring Malaya.

625 g (1¼ lb) lean beef or lamb steak, cut into thin strips
3 tablespoons sunflower oil
4 or 5 spring onion bulbs, chopped
2 lemon grass stalks, fresh or bottled, chopped finely
150 ml (¼ pint) chicken stock
5 or 6 whole lime leaves, fresh or dried
4 tablespoons coconut milk powder
227 g can of sliced bamboo shoots, liquid reserved
3 tablespoons minced sweet basil
1 tablespoon minced coriander

salt
For the paste:
1 teaspoon Thai red curry paste
2 teaspoons minced garlic
4 teaspoons minced sweet basil
4 or 5 spring onions, leaves only, chopped
4 tablespoons peanut butter
1 tablespoon tomato ketchup
1 teaspoon brown sugar
1 teaspoon chilli powder
2 tablespoons chopped red pepper
25 g (1 oz) small cooked, peeled prawns (optional)

❶ Cut the meat into thin strips, ideally about 5 cm (2 inches) × 2.5 cm (1 inch) × 5 mm (¼ inch). It is easier to cut the meat thinly if it is still almost frozen.

❷ Put the paste ingredients into a food processor and process, adding enough water to make a thick paste.

❸ Heat the oil in a wok until it is quite hot. Add the onions and the meat, and stir-fry briskly for 2 or 3 minutes.

❹ Add the paste and lemon grass and stir-fry continuously for a further 3 minutes.

❺ Add the stock and lime leaves. Simmer and stir for about 3 more minutes.

❻ Add the remaining ingredients and continue to stir-fry for 2 or 3 minutes more or until the meat is as tender as you like it.

Thai Red Curry Rice

Preparation and cooking time: 10 minutes.
Freezing: recommended. Serves 4.

1 tablespoon sunflower oil
2 teaspoons minced garlic
1 teaspoon Thai red curry paste
1 teaspoon minced sweet basil
1 teaspoon chopped red pepper
1 or 2 whole red chillies, de-seeded and
   chopped finely (optional)

2 or 3 spring onions, chopped finely
125 g (4 oz) canned mixed Chinese
   vegetables, chopped
500 g (1 lb) cooked rice
1 tablespoon chopped fresh basil
salt

❶ Heat the oil in a wok until it is quite hot. Add the garlic, curry paste, sweet basil, red pepper, chillies and onions. Stir-fry for about 2 minutes.
❷ Add the vegetables, and when hot, add the cold rice.

❸ Briskly, but gently (taking care not to break the grains of rice), stir-fry everything until it is hot.
❹ Add the fresh basil and season with salt.

Chicken Thai Green Curry

Preparation time: 10 minutes + 20 minutes cooking.
Freezing: recommended. Serves 4.

This green curry, fragrant with herbs and creamy with coconut gravy, is probably Thailand's best known dish.

500 g (1 lb) chicken breast stir-fry fillets
4 tablespoons sunflower oil
200 ml (7 fl oz) canned coconut milk
2 lemon grass stalks, chopped finely
2 or 3 lime leaves
5 or 6 spring onion bulbs, chopped
125 g (4 oz) fresh mange tout, halved
125 g (4 oz) frozen peas
1 tablespoon chopped fresh basil

salt
For the paste:
1 teaspoon Thai green curry paste
1 teaspoon minced coriander
1 teaspoon minced basil
2 teaspoons minced garlic
1 teaspoon minced ginger
5 or 6 spring onions, leaves only, chopped
1 green pepper, de-seeded and chopped

❶ In a food processor, blend the ingredients for the paste.
❷ Cut the chicken into 2 cm (¾-inch) cubes.
❸ Heat the oil in a wok until it is quite hot. Add the paste and stir-fry for about 2 minutes.
❹ Add the coconut milk, lemon grass and lime leaves. Stir-fry for 3 or 4 minutes.

❺ Add the onions and the chicken and stir-fry briskly for about 5 minutes more.
❻ Add the mange tout and peas and continue to stir-fry for about 5 minutes.
❼ Add the basil and bring to the simmer.
❽ Check that the chicken is cooked by cutting a piece in half. It should be white all the way through. If not, continue stir-frying until it is. Season with salt.

Pork Satays in Peanut Sauce

Preparation time: 10 minutes + 15 minutes cooking + marinating (optional).
Freezing: recommended. Serves 4 as a starter.

One of Thailand's speciality starters is the satay. Meat is marinated in a peanut and chilli sauce and then grilled on a skewer. Here the dish is modified to become a quick-and-easy stir-fry. Serve with chilli sauce and salad.

400 g (13 oz) frozen lean pork steak

75 g (3 oz) peanut butter

3 tablespoons sweet chilli sauce

1 tablespoon tomato ketchup

2 teaspoons soy sauce

2 tablespoons soya or sunflower oil

1 teaspoon minced garlic

4 or 5 spring onion bulbs, chopped finely

salt

❶ Cut the meat into thin strips, ideally about 5 cm (2 inches) × 2.5 cm (1 inch) × 5 mm (¼ inch). It is easier to cut meat thinly if it is still almost frozen.

❷ Mix the peanut butter, chilli sauce, tomato ketchup and soy sauce together in a large bowl, adding just enough water to make it run off the spoon. Add the meat strips, making sure that they are well coated with the mixture. If you have time, you can cover the bowl and refrigerate it for up to 24 hours or you can cook the meat at once.

❸ Heat the oil until it is quite hot. Add the garlic and stir-fry for about 30 seconds. Add the onions and continue to stir-fry for 2 or 3 minutes more.

❹ Add the meat, shaking off excess marinade into the bowl. Stir-fry briskly for at least 5 minutes, turning the meat regularly. To prevent it from sticking to the wok, add splashes of water, as necessary.

❺ Add the remaining marinade, and keep on stir-frying for a further 4–6 minutes, until the meat is cooked. Season with salt. Serve hot or cold.

Duck and Orange Stir-fry Salad

Preparation time: 10 minutes + 10 minutes cooking + 1 hour chilling.
Freezing: not recommended. Serves 4.

No Thai meal would be complete without its meat, poultry or seafood salad. First garlic, herbs and other aromatic ingredients are stir-fried. These will flavour the main ingredient – in this case it's duck. Serve the salad, chilled, as a starter or with the main meal.

200 g (7 oz) boneless, skinless duck breast

2 tablespoons sesame or sunflower oil

1 teaspoon minced sweet basil

2 teaspoons minced garlic

2 lemon grass stalks, bottled or fresh,
    chopped finely

2 or 3 lime leaves, dried or fresh

2–3 spring onions, chopped

150 ml (¼ pint) vegetable stock or water

1 tablespoon coconut milk powder

200 g packet of mixed salad leaves, chopped

50 g (2 oz) fresh chopped basil

25 g (1 oz) fresh chopped coriander

4–6 tangerines, peeled and divided into
    segments

salt

❶ Cut the duck into thin strips, ideally about 5 cm (2 inches) × 2.5 cm (1 inch) × 3 mm (⅛ inch) thick. It is easier to cut meat thinly if it is still almost frozen.

❷ Heat the oil in a wok. Add the basil, garlic, lemon grass, lime leaves and onions. Stir-fry for 1 minute.

❸ Add the stock and when it is simmering, add the duck. Stir-fry for the least possible time to cook the duck to your liking (at least 5 minutes).

❹ Stir in the coconut powder. Transfer the stir-fry to a large salad bowl, and let it cool.

❺ Add the salad leaves, herbs and tangerine segments.

❻ Mix everything together in the salad bowl and season with salt.

❼ Cover and refrigerate for an hour.

Pad Thai

Preparation time: 5 minutes + 10 minutes cooking. Freezing: not recommended. Serves 4.

Pad Thai literally means 'Thai stir-fry'. This is Thailand's most celebrated noodle dish.

50 g (2 oz) chicken breast stir-fry fillets, cut
   into thin strips
125 g (4 oz) rice noodles
2 tablespoons sunflower oil
1 teaspoon Thai red curry paste
2 teaspoons minced garlic
1 teaspoon minced ginger
125 ml (4 fl oz) sweet and sour sauce
2 lemon grass stalks, fresh or bottled,
   chopped finely

5 or 6 lime leaves, fresh or dried
5 or 6 spring onions, chopped
1 tablespoon chopped red pepper
1 tablespoon chopped yellow pepper
1 or 2 whole red chillies, de-seeded and
   chopped finely
50 g (2 oz) small cooked, peeled prawns
200 ml (7 fl oz) chicken or fish stock
3 tablespoons minced sweet basil
salt

❶ Bring a saucepan of water to the boil. Immerse the noodles. Bring the water back to the boil. Simmer for 2 or 3 minutes, then turn off the heat. Put on the lid and leave the noodles for 5 or 6 minutes. Drain and keep warm.

❷ Heat the oil in a wok until it is quite hot. Add the curry paste, garlic and ginger and stir-fry for about 30 seconds. Add the chicken, sweet and sour sauce, lemon grass, lime leaves, onions, peppers and chillies. Continue to stir-fry for about 2 minutes more.

❸ Add the prawns and the stock, and stir-fry while it simmers for about 3 minutes.

❹ Add the basil, then the noodles, very carefully stirring them into the wok ingredients.

❺ When everything is hot, season with salt and serve.

Indian Stir-fries

Indian food is arguably the most savoury in the world. It is undeniably the spiciest. We do not normally think stir-fry when we think Indian, yet one of India's most versatile cooking pots is the karahi or balti pan. It is used for boiling, steaming, deep-frying and stir-frying. If you don't have such a pan, the wok is just as suitable. My brief selection includes two starters, Spicy Liver and Jeera Chicken, and two classics, a korma from centuries ago, and tikka masala, recently invented in the British Indian restaurant. Though neither would normally be cooked by stir-frying, they are here in specially modified recipes. Balti is by definition a stir-fry, as is the delicious Seasonal Vegetable Curry. My other stir-fry adaptations are a Red Bean, Green Pea and Chick-pea Curry, and pullao rice.

Seasonal Vegetable Curry

**Preparation time: 10 minutes + 10 minutes cooking.
Freezing: not recommended. Serves 4.**

Nowhere do vegetables taste better than in Indian cooking. Here you can choose what you use, so you can take advantage of what is in season.

625 g (1¼ lb) selection of seasonal
   vegetables, chopped
2 tablespoons vegetable oil
1 teaspoon mustard seeds
2 teaspoons minced garlic
½ teaspoon turmeric
½ teaspoon chilli powder

1 teaspoon mustard powder
2 or 3 leeks, chopped into rings
125 g (4 oz) rocket, chopped
1 tablespoon desiccated coconut
1 tablespoon finely chopped fresh coriander
   leaves
salt

❶ Blanch or microwave the vegetables so that they are cooked but still crisp. Keep hot.

❷ Heat the oil in a wok or karahi. Add the mustard seeds, and garlic and stir-fry for about 30 seconds. Add the turmeric, chilli powder, and mustard powder with 4 tablespoons of water. Stir-fry for a further 2 minutes.

❸ Add the leeks and the seasonal vegetables. Stir-fry for about 3 minutes.

❹ Add the remaining ingredients, with just enough water to keep things from sticking. Stir-fry for about 2 more minutes and serve.

Meat Korma Curry

Preparation time: 10 minutes + 35 minutes cooking.
Freezing: recommended. Serves 4.

Normally this mild and creamy curry would be cooked slowly in a saucepan, but I have modified the recipe to make it a relatively quick stir-fry. Serve with the Special Mixed Pullao Rice on page 38.

625 g (1¼ lb) lean lamb or veal steak

3 tablespoons vegetable ghee or oil

1 teaspoon fennel seeds

4 or 5 crushed green cardamoms

4 or 5 crushed cloves

1 teaspoon cinnamon powder

1 teaspoon ground coriander

½ teaspoon chilli powder

½ teaspoon turmeric

2 teaspoons minced garlic

2 teaspoons minced ginger

1 teaspoon mild or medium curry paste

175 g (6 oz) spring onions, chopped

150 ml (¼ pint) milk

200 ml (7 fl oz) crème fraîche

50 g (2 oz) creamed coconut, chopped

1 tablespoon chopped fresh coriander

1 to 2 teaspoons garam masala

2 tablespoons ground almonds

salt

❶ Cut the meat into 1 cm (½-inch) cubes.

❷ Heat half the ghee, or oil, in a heavy-based saucepan. Add the meat and stir-fry for about 5 minutes. At the end of this time remove from the heat, but keep warm.

❸ Heat the remaining ghee or oil in a wok or karahi. Add the fennel seeds, cardamoms, cloves, cinnamon, ground coriander, chilli and turmeric. Stir-fry for about 30 seconds. Add the garlic and stir-fry for a further 30 seconds. Add the ginger and stir-fry for a further 30 seconds. Add the curry paste and stir-fry for a further minute.

❹ Add 4 tablespoons of water, and when it sizzles, add the onions. Stir-fry for about 4 minutes.

❺ Add the contents of the wok to the meat cubes in the saucepan, return to the heat, and when sizzling, add the milk little by little over the next 5 minutes until it is reduced to a creamy gravy.

❻ Lower the heat and add the crème fraîche and creamed coconut, stirring gently but thoroughly for about 5 minutes as it dissolves and amalgamates with the mixture.

❼ Raise the heat so that the curry sizzles, and stir from time to time for a further 10 minutes, gradually adding just enough water to prevent sticking.

❽ Add the fresh coriander, garam masala and ground almonds.

❾ Continue to cook, stirring and adding water as necessary. Test the meat but it probably needs to cook for at least 10 minutes more until it is tender.

❿ Season with salt. Garnish and serve.

Spicy Liver

Preparation time: 5 minutes + 15 minutes cooking.
Freezing: recommended. Serves 4 as a starter.

This is one of India's really delightful stir-fry starters, and it's so simple.
Serve with a yogurt dip, Indian bread and a salad.

375 g (12 oz) lamb's liver

2 tablespoons sunflower oil

2 teaspoons cumin seeds

2 teaspoons minced garlic

4–6 spring onions, chopped

2 teaspoons paprika

2 tablespoons tomato ketchup

1 or 2 tablespoons sweet chilli sauce

salt

❶ Cut the liver into 2 cm (¾-inch) cubes.
❷ Heat the oil in a wok until it is quite hot. Add the cumin and garlic and stir-fry for about 30 seconds. Add the onions and paprika and continue to stir-fry for 2 or 3 minutes more.

❸ Add the liver, and stir gently from time to time, for about 5 minutes.
❹ Add the ketchup and chilli sauce. Continue to stir-fry for a further 5 minutes or so, ensuring the liver is tender but cooked right through. Season with salt.

Red Bean, Green Pea and Chick-pea Curry

Preparation and cooking time: 15 minutes.
Freezing: recommended. Serves 4.

This delicious curry is superb simply with plain rice or Indian bread.

4 tablespoons ghee or vegetable oil

2 tablespoons medium or mild curry paste

2 teaspoons minced ginger

5 or 6 spring onions, chopped

1 or 2 red chillies, de-seeded and chopped
  finely (optional)

420 g can of red kidney beans, drained and
  rinsed

420 g can of chick-peas, drained and rinsed,
  liquid reserved

1 tablespoon tomato purée

100 g (3½ oz) houmous

6 tablespoons greek-style yogurt

125 g (4 oz) garden peas

1 teaspoon garam masala

salt

To garnish:

lime wedges

fresh coriander

❶ Heat the ghee or oil in a wok or karahi. Add the curry paste and stir-fry for about 30 seconds. Add the ginger and continue to stir-fry for 30 seconds more.
❷ Add 4 tablespoons of water, and when it is sizzling, add the onions and chillies. Stir-fry for about 4 minutes.
❸ Add the beans, chick-peas and

remaining ingredients. Stir-fry for about 4 more minutes, during which time you may wish to add in some, or all of the chick-pea liquid, depending on how runny you wish your curry to be. Season with salt. Garnish with the lime wedges and coriander, and serve.

Chicken and Mushroom Balti

Preparation time: 10 minutes + 20 minutes cooking.
Freezing: recommended. Serves 4.

Baltis are the stir-fries of the curry house and as such they should be fresh, aromatic, spicy, herby and thoroughly delicious. Serve with naan bread and chutneys.

4 tablespoons vegetable ghee or oil

1 teaspoon cumin seeds

1 teaspoon fennel seeds

1 teaspoon mustard seeds

2 teaspoons minced garlic

2 teaspoons minced ginger

1 tablespoon mild or medium curry paste

1 teaspoon garam masala

4–6 spring onions, chopped

500 g (1 lb) chicken breast stir-fry fillets, cut into 2 cm (¾-inch) cubes

1 black or green pepper, de-seeded and chopped

1 red pepper, de-seeded and chopped

1 or 2 fresh green cayenne chillies, de-seeded and chopped finely

250 g (8 oz) mushrooms, sliced lengthways

12 mint leaves, chopped

2 tablespoons chopped fresh coriander

1 tablespoon tomato ketchup

1 teaspoon Worcestershire sauce

4 canned plum tomatoes, chopped

salt

❶ Heat the ghee or oil in a wok or karahi. Add the cumin, fennel and mustard seeds. Add the garlic and stir-fry for about 30 seconds. Add the ginger and stir-fry for a further 30 seconds. Add the curry paste and garam masala and continue to stir-fry for 2 minutes.

❷ Add 4 tablespoons of water, and when it is sizzling, add the onions. Stir-fry for about 4 minutes.

❸ Add the chicken, and stir occasionally over the next 4 minutes.

❹ Add the peppers and chillies and enough water to keep things from sticking. Stir-fry for a further 4 minutes.

❺ Add the mushrooms, herbs, tomato ketchup, Worcestershire sauce and tomatoes. Stir-fry for about 4 more minutes.

❻ Check that the chicken is cooked right through by cutting a piece in half. It should be white all the way through. If not, continue stir-frying until it is. Season with salt.

Special Mixed Pullao Rice

Preparation and cooking time: 10 minutes.
Freezing: recommended. Serves 4.

2 tablespoons ghee or vegetable oil

1 teaspoon mild or medium curry paste

500 g (1 lb) cooked rice

1 tablespoon ground almonds

1 tablespoon tomato purée

1 tablespoon coconut milk powder

4 tablespoons canned sweetcorn

salt

❶ Heat the ghee or oil in a wok or karahi until it is quite hot. Add the curry paste and stir-fry for about 30 seconds.

❷ Add the cold rice and remaining ingredients. Briskly but gently (so as not to break up the grains of rice), stir-fry everything until it is heated through.

❸ Season with salt and serve.

Jeera Chicken

Preparation time: 5 minutes + 15 minutes cooking.
Freezing: recommended. Serves 4 as a starter.

This tasty stir-fry from the Punjab uses both whole and ground jeera (cumin). Serve hot or cold with Indian bread, salad and chutneys.

500 g (1 lb) boneless, skinless chicken breast

50 g (2 oz) butter

1 tablespoon cumin seeds

2 tablespoons ground cumin

300 ml (½ pint) chicken stock or water

salt

❶ Cut the chicken into 2 cm (¾-inch) cubes.

❷ Heat the butter in a wok until it is quite hot – be careful not to burn it. Add the cumin seeds and stir-fry for about 30 seconds. Add the ground cumin and continue to stir-fry for about 2 or 3 minutes more.

❸ Add the chicken pieces, and stir-fry briskly for about 2 minutes. Then lower the heat a little, and over the next 5 minutes add the remaining stock or water, stirring as necessary.

❹ Turn up the heat and resume stirring briskly for about 5 more minutes to reduce the remaining liquid to form a gravy which coats the chicken.

❺ Check that the chicken is cooked all the way through by cutting a piece in half. It should be white right through. If not, continue stir-frying until it is. Season with salt.

King Prawn Tikka Masala

Preparation time: 10 minutes + 20 minutes cooking.
Freezing: recommended. Serves 4.

Britain's most popular curry is delicious with king prawns. You could also try using chicken – just cook it 10 minutes longer in step 4.

625 g (1¼ lb) peeled, cooked king prawns
  (the larger the better)
4 tablespoons vegetable ghee or oil
1 teaspoon cumin seeds
1 teaspoon fennel seeds
2 teaspoons minced garlic
2 tablespoons tandoori paste
1 tablespoon mild or medium curry paste
4–6 spring onions, chopped
1 red pepper, chopped
1–3 green chillies, de-seeded and chopped
  finely

1 tablespoon tomato purée
1 tablespoon tomato ketchup
4 or 5 canned plum tomatoes
1 tablespoon chopped fresh mint
1 tablespoon chopped fresh coriander
1 teaspoon garam masala
1 teaspoon sugar
3 tablespoons double cream
salt

❶ De-vein the king prawns by cutting along the back and removing the vein. Wash and dry them.

❷ Heat the ghee or oil in a wok or karahi. Add the cumin, fennel seeds, and garlic and stir-fry for about 30 seconds. Add the tandoori and curry pastes and stir-fry for a further 2 minutes.

❸ Add 4 tablespoons of water and when this is sizzling add the onions. Stir-fry for about 1 minute.

❹ Add the pepper, chillies, tomato purée, ketchup and tomatoes. Add enough water to keep things from sticking. Stir-fry for a further 4 minutes.

❺ Add the king prawns, and stir from time to time for about 4 minutes.

❻ Add the remaining ingredients. Stir-fry for about 4 more minutes and serve.

American Stir-fries

From America comes Chicken Maryland, that perfect marriage of chicken and sweetcorn represented here with a simple stir-fry; and there's the delicious, really simple Caramelised Sweetcorn. Considerably more spicy are three fabulous Cajun and Creole dishes from Louisiana: gumbo, jambalaya, and blackened scampi. The Caribbean is represented by a simple stir-fry of chilli meat and vegetables and the ever-popular rice and peas.

Blackened Scampi or King Prawns

Preparation time: 5 minutes + 10 minutes cooking.
Freezing: recommended. Serves 2.

For the authentic Cajun version of this dish, crawfish or miniature lobsters (which we call crayfish) are used. Scampi or large king prawns are usually more readily available at the fish counter. Enjoy them with salad, rice or hot crusty garlic bread, and some ice-cold lager.

8 raw shell-on crayfish, each about 15 cm
   (6-inches) long or 16 raw shell-on fresh
   scampi or large king prawns
4 tablespoons butter
oil, for brushing
lemon wedges, to serve

For the coating:
3 tablespoons cornflour
1 teaspoon black pepper
1 teaspoon mustard powder
1 teaspoon ground cumin
1 teaspoon paprika
1 teaspoon salt

❶ Peel the scampi, king prawns or crayfish. Keep the tails on, if you wish. De-vein, wash and dry them thoroughly.

❷ Brush them all over with the oil.

❸ Mix the coating ingredients together in a flat bowl.

❹ Dab the shellfish in the coating mixture until they are evenly coated.

❺ Heat the butter in a flat frying-pan. Fry the shellfish for about 3–4 minutes, stirring as needed.

❻ Turn them over and repeat.

❼ Check that they are cooked, by cutting into one. It should be evenly cooked all the way through. Serve piping hot with the lemon wedges.

Turkey and Okra Gumbo Creole

Preparation time: 5 minutes + 20 minutes cooking.
Freezing: recommended. Serves 4.

Gumbo was originally a stew made by American slaves, but now it is
'haute-cuisine' in fashionable restaurants. To be authentic, it must
contain gooey okra, as it does in this tasty stir-fry. Serve with rice and
potatoes.

200 g (7 oz) boneless, skinless turkey breasts

2 tablespoons corn oil

2 tablespoons cornflour

1.2 litres (2 pints) chicken stock

2 tablespoons butter

2 teaspoons minced garlic

1 red chilli, de-seeded and chopped finely

4 to 6 spring onions, chopped

1 tablespoon chopped red pepper

1 tablespoon chopped green pepper

1 tablespoon chopped fresh thyme

150 g (5 oz) fresh okra, chopped

24 canned or bottled oysters, or fresh oysters, shelled

175 g tub of peeled prawns in brine

3 or 4 tablespoons American rye whisky

salt

❶ Cut the turkey into 2 cm (¾-inch) cubes.

❷ Heat the oil in a wok. Add the flour little by little until it is mixed in. Continue cooking just long enough to brown it. Lower the heat, then little by little, add the stock, stirring diligently to prevent it from forming lumps. Continue until it is fully combined and has finished thickening.

❸ Heat the butter in another wok. Stir-fry the garlic and chilli for 30 seconds. Add the onion, red and green pepper and turkey chunks. Continue to stir-fry for 3–4 minutes.

❹ Transfer the stir-fry to the wok with the sauce, and simmer for 8 minutes stirring from time to time.

❺ Add the okra to the wok. Add the remaining ingredients including some of the prawn brine, both to season your dish and to keep things from sticking to the pan.

❻ When everything is hot, check that the turkey is cooked right through by cutting a piece in half. It should be the same colour all the way through. If not, continue cooking until it is. Season with salt and serve.

Rice and Peas

Preparation and cooking time: 15 minutes.
Freezing: recommended. Serves 4.

2 tablespoons olive oil

2 or 3 streaky bacon rashers, chopped

2 teaspoons minced garlic

1 chilli, de-seeded and chopped finely (optional)

3 or 4 spring onions, chopped

1 tablespoon chopped red pepper

1 tablespoon chopped green pepper

1 tablespoon sun-dried tomatoes, chopped

1 teaspoon green peppercorns in brine

300 g (10 oz) cooked rice

432 g can of yellow split peas

salt

❶ Heat the oil in a wok until it is quite hot. Add the bacon, and stir-fry for a couple of minutes. Add the garlic and chilli and stir-fry for about 30 seconds. Add the onions, red and green peppers, tomatoes and peppercorns. Stir-fry for about 2 minutes.

❷ Add the cooled rice and split peas. Briskly, but gently (so as not to break up the grains of rice), stir-fry everything until it is hot.

❸ Season with salt and serve.

Chicken Maryland

Preparation time: 10 minutes + 20 minutes cooking.
Freezing: recommended. Serves 4.

This is a simple version of an American East Coast favourite. Serve with rice or potatoes.

625 g (1¼ lb) chicken breast stir-fry fillets

1 tablespoon corn oil

1 tablespoon cornflour

300 ml (½ pint) milk

3 tablespoons butter

2 streaky bacon rashers, chopped

1 teaspoon minced garlic

1 green chilli, de-seeded and chopped finely (optional)

5 or 6 spring onions, chopped

2 tablespoons chopped red pepper

300 g (10 oz) creamed sweetcorn

salt

parsley, to garnish

❶ Cut the chicken into 2 cm (¾-inch) cubes.

❷ Heat the oil in a wok. Add the cornflour little by little until it has all blended into the oil. Lower the heat, then little by little add the milk, stirring diligently to prevent it from getting lumpy. Continue until it is fully combined and has finished thickening.

❸ Heat the butter in another wok. Stir-fry the bacon until it starts to go crisp. Add the garlic and chilli and stir-fry for 30 seconds.

❹ Add the chicken, onions and pepper. Continue to stir-fry for about 3–4 minutes.

❺ Add the stir-fry to the milk and cornflour sauce and simmer for about 8 minutes, stirring from time to time.

❻ Add the sweetcorn, and stir until it is hot. Season with salt.

❼ Check that the chicken is cooked right through by cutting a piece in half. It should be white all the way through. If not, continue stir-frying until it is.

❽ Garnish with the parsley.

Caribbean Chilli Meat and Vegetables

Preparation time: 10 minutes + 20 minutes cooking.
Freezing: recommended. Serves 4.

They like it hot in the West Indies – both their weather and their chillies! They use the extra-hot scotch bonnet or habanero chillies to fire up kid or goat meat, plantains and gourds. If these chillies are a little too strong for you, try a milder variety such as Dutch red.

625 g (1¼ lb) lean veal steak
2 tablespoons olive oil
2 teaspoons minced garlic
1 scotch bonnet yellow or red chilli, chopped finely
1 teaspoon crushed coriander seeds
4 bay leaves
200 g (7 oz) onion, chopped
2 tablespoons chopped green pepper
75 g (3 oz) sun-dried tomatoes in oil, chopped

1 or 2 celery sticks, chopped
1 plantain or firm banana, chopped (optional)
1 small marrow or 2 courgettes, chopped
1 or 2 teaspoons green peppercorns in brine
200 ml (7 fl oz) meat or vegetable stock
4 tablespoons rum
1 teaspoon ground mace
1 tablespoon chopped fresh coriander
salt

❶ Cut the meat into thin strips, ideally about 5 cm (2 inches) × 2.5 cm (1 inch) × 5 mm (¼ inch). (It is easier to cut meat thinly if it is still almost frozen.)

❷ Heat the oil in a wok. Stir-fry the coriander seeds, bay leaves, garlic and chilli for 30 seconds. Add the onion, pepper, sun-dried tomatoes and celery, and continue to stir-fry for 3–4 minutes.

❸ Peel and chop the banana or plantain and the marrow or courgettes and add to the pan.

❹ When they are sizzling, add the peppercorns, 1 teaspoon of peppercorn in brine and the meat. Stir-fry briskly for about 3 minutes, to seal the meat.

❺ Add the stock and simmer for about 8 minutes.

❻ Add the remaining ingredients. Simmer for 3 minutes more and serve.

Caramelised Sweetcorn

Preparation and cooking time: 15 minutes.
Freezing: recommended. Serves 4 as a starter.

I stumbled on this recipe years ago when I forgot that the contents of my frying-pan were cooking away merrily. When I did remember, I expected burnt offerings. To my surprise, the sugar in the sweetcorn had caramelised perfectly and only needed a final stir-fry! This is delicious as a starter, or as a vegetable side dish. Be sure to use the normal canned sweetcorn, and not the 'light' kind, and cook exactly as instructed.

3 tablespoons unsalted butter

326 g can of sweetcorn kernels, drained

❶ Heat the butter in a large frying-pan on a fairly low heat.

❷ Add the sweetcorn. Stir-fry for about 30 seconds and then pat it down with the spoon so that it covers the pan.

❸ Leave it cooking quietly for about 15 minutes. It should have caramelised so that some kernels turn a deep golden brown.

❹ Use the spoon to unstick the kernels and turn them over. Then stir-fry for a few more minutes. Serve hot. There is no need to add salt.

Jambalaya

Preparation time: 10 minutes + 10 minutes cooking.
Freezing: recommended. Serves 4.

The beauty of this substantial Cajun dish is that you can use just about any ingredient you like, providing you include rice and ham.

2 tablespoons corn oil
2 teaspoons minced garlic
1 or 2 green chillies, de-seeded and chopped finely
2 or 3 spring onions, chopped
1 tablespoon chopped red pepper
1 tablespoon chopped yellow pepper

300 g (10 oz) mixed cooked ham, pork, chicken, turkey, chorizo, salami, prawns
1 tablespoon chopped fresh oregano
175 ml (6 fl oz) vegetable stock
60 ml (2 fl oz) sherry
500 g (1 lb) cooked rice
salt and freshly ground black pepper

❶ Heat the oil in a wok. Stir-fry the garlic and chilli for 30 seconds. Add the onions and red and yellow pepper. Continue to stir-fry for 3–4 minutes.

❷ Cut the cooked meat into small strips if necessary. Add the cooked meat or prawns to the wok and stir-fry for a couple of minutes more.

❸ Add the oregano, stock and sherry. Bring to a simmer and add the rice. Briskly but gently (so as not to break up the grains of rice), stir-fry everything until it is hot. Season with salt and pepper.

Mexican Stir-fries
Chilli is actually an American invention, and the recipe here hails from New Mexico. The other recipes in this chapter are authentic Mexican creations. Many of the ingredients are those which the Spanish conquistadors discovered in Mexico 500 years ago, such as sweetcorn, avocados, potatoes, beans, turkey, chocolate, sweet peppers, and of course, chillies.

Tex-Mex Chilli Beans

Preparation time: 5 minutes + 30 minutes cooking.
Freezing: recommended. Serves 4.

This is actually from New Mexico in the USA. Serve with crusty hot garlic bread and some ice-cold beer.

2 tablespoons corn oil

2 teaspoons minced garlic

½ teaspoon cumin seeds

½ teaspoon ground cumin

2 or 3 green chillies, de-seeded and chopped finely

4–6 spring onions, chopped

2 tablespoons chopped red pepper

375 g (12 oz) lean mince

1 teaspoon vinegar

1 tablespoon tomato paste

1 tablespoon tomato ketchup

4 or 5 canned plum tomatoes

420 g canned red kidney beans, drained and rinsed

2 tablespoons chopped fresh coriander

salt

❶ Heat the oil in a wok. Stir-fry the garlic, cumin seeds, ground cumin and chillies for 30 seconds. Add the onions and red pepper. Continue to stir-fry for 3–4 minutes.

❷ Add the mince, and stir-fry for about 5 minutes.

❸ Lower the heat, add the vinegar and the tomato paste, tomato ketchup, and canned tomatoes. Simmer for about 15 minutes, stirring from time to time.

❹ Add the beans and coriander. Cook for a further 5 minutes and then season with salt.

Fajitas Tacos

Preparation and cooking time: 20 minutes + marinating.
Freezing: recommended. Serves 4.

This is a very popular Mexican dish, which makes a substantial snack.
Use an oaky New World red wine for the marinade and enjoy a glass or
two with the Fajitas.

500 g (1 lb) lean beef steak

2 tablespoons corn oil

4 garlic cloves, chopped finely

½ teaspoon cumin seeds

1 green chilli, de-seeded and chopped finely

2 or 3 spring onions, chopped

1 tablespoon chopped red pepper

1 tablespoon chopped green pepper

225 g canned re-fried beans

8 soft tortillas

100 ml (3½ fl oz) soured cream

salt

ready-made chilli salsa sauce, to serve

For the marinade:

90 ml (3 fl oz) red wine

60 ml (2 fl oz) tequila (optional)

2 tablespoons wine vinegar

❶ Cut the meat into thin strips, ideally about 5 cm (2 inches) × 2.5 cm (1 inch) × 5 mm (¼ inch). It is easier to cut meat thinly if it is still almost frozen.

❷ Mix the ingredients for the marinade together. Add the meat to the marinade and leave for at least 30 minutes. If you have time, cover and marinate in the fridge all day or overnight, for up to 24 hours.

❸ Heat the oil in a wok. Stir-fry the garlic, cumin and chilli for 30 seconds. Add the onion, red and green peppers and continue to stir-fry for a couple more minutes. Add the re-fried beans and mix in well. Continue to cook until heated through.

❹ In another wok or frying-pan, add the meat. Stir-fry for about 5 minutes, or until cooked to your liking. Season with salt.

❺ To serve, place a tortilla on a serving plate. Top with some meat, followed by the re-fried beans and a dollop of soured cream. Fold the tortilla over. Serve with some ready-made chilli salsa sauce.

Ocapa Avocado Queso

Preparation time: 10 minutes + 20 minutes cooking.
Freezing: not recommended. Serves 4.

Nothing tastes better than the humble potato when it is incorporated into a tasty sauce, such as this one with avocado and cream cheese.

500 g (1 lb) baby new potatoes

2 tablespoons butter

1 tablespoon chopped fresh oregano

2 tablespoons corn oil

1 teaspoon minced garlic

1 red chilli, de-seeded and chopped finely

3 or 4 spring onions, chopped

125 ml (4 fl oz) soured cream

125 g (4 oz) cream cheese

1 very ripe avocado, mashed

a handful of grated Cheddar cheese

salt and freshly ground black pepper

❶ Cook the potatoes. Drain, add the butter and fresh oregano. Keep warm.

❷ Heat the oil in a wok. Stir-fry the garlic and chilli for 30 seconds. Add the onions and continue to stir-fry for 3–4 minutes.

❸ Add the soured cream, cream cheese and avocado. Stir-fry for 2–3 minutes to allow it to thicken a little.

❹ Put the hot potatoes into a serving bowl. Pour the sauce over them, mixing well. Season with salt and pepper and sprinkle over the cheese. Serve hot.

Chorizo and Green Bean Chilli

Preparation time: 10 minutes + 10 minutes cooking.
Freezing: recommended. Serves 4.

Fabulous Mexican tastes and textures. Enjoy this with a baked potato and soured cream. And keep some of the tequila to enjoy with the meal too!

2 tablespoons olive oil

2 teaspoons minced garlic

1 teaspoon ground cumin

1 red chilli, de-seeded and chopped finely

3 or 4 spring onions, chopped

6 pitted black olives, quartered

2 tablespoons chopped green pepper

325 g (11 oz) fresh Kenyan beans, chopped

125 g (4 oz) celery, chopped finely

300 g (10 oz) chorizo, skinned and chopped

150 g (5 oz) fresh guacamole

1 tablespoon chopped fresh sorrel

60 ml (2 fl oz) tequila or sherry

salt

❶ Heat the oil in a wok. Stir-fry the garlic, cumin and chilli for 30 seconds. Add the onions, olives and green peppers. Continue to stir-fry for 3–4 minutes.

❷ Cook the beans: drop into a saucepan of boiling water and cook for 2–3 minutes or microwave so that beans are just cooked and still retain their crunchy texture.

❸ Add the beans, celery and chorizo to the wok. Stir-fry for a couple of minutes.

❹ Add the guacamole, sorrel and, when hot, stir in the tequila. Season with salt and serve at once.

Huevos Rancheros

Preparation time: 5 minutes + 10 minutes cooking.
Freezing: not recommended. Serves 2.

The name of this dish means 'ranchers' eggs'. Mexico has its cowboys too, and this, they say, is their favourite dish. It makes a tasty stir-fry starter or snack.

2 tablespoons olive oil

2 garlic cloves, chopped finely

½ teaspoon cumin seeds

1 teaspoon finely chopped red chilli

2 or 3 spring onions, chopped

1 tablespoon chopped purple pepper

1 tablespoon chopped yellow pepper

4 tortillas

2 tablespoons butter

4 eggs

4 large pitted green olives, quartered

4 cherry tomatoes, halved

2 tablespoons mild or hot taco sauce

1 tablespoon sweetcorn relish

1 teaspoon sun-dried tomato paste

1 tablespoon chopped fresh oregano

1 teaspoon green peppercorns in brine, crushed

salt

To garnish:

freshly ground black pepper

snipped chives

❶ Heat the oil in a wok. Stir-fry the garlic, cumin seeds and chilli for 30 seconds. Add the onions and purple and yellow peppers. Continue to stir-fry for 3–4 minutes.

❷ Put the tortillas on two serving plates.

❸ Heat the butter in a frying-pan, and fry the eggs.

❹ While the eggs are frying, add the remaining ingredients to the wok and stir-fry for about 5 minutes to create the sauce. Season with salt.

❺ Drizzle the sauce over the tortillas, and place an egg on top of each one. Garnish with some freshly ground pepper and the chives.

Turkey and Corn Molé

Preparation time: 10 minutes + 20 minutes cooking.
Freezing: recommended. Serves 4.

This remarkable dish combines turkey, sweetcorn, chilli and chocolate – four ingredients indigenous to Mexico. Chocolate? Yes, chocolate! And be sure to use it; once you've tried it, you'll be hooked! Serve with salsas, blue tortilla chips and plain rice, and a red Rioja wine.

625 g (1¼ lb) skinless turkey leg or breast

3 tablespoons corn oil

2 teaspoons minced garlic

1–3 teaspoons chilli powder

½ teaspoon ground coriander

½ teaspoon ground cumin

125 g (4 oz) onion, chopped finely

1 tablespoon finely chopped black or green pepper

1 tablespoon sun-dried tomato paste

200 g (7 oz) canned chopped tomatoes with herbs

1 tablespoon chopped fresh coriander

1 tablespoon brown sugar

1 tablespoon ground almonds

10 blue tortilla chips, crumbled finely

50 g (2 oz) dark or bitter chocolate, chopped

salt

❶ Cut the turkey into 2 cm (¾-inch) cubes.

❷ Heat the oil in a wok. Stir-fry the garlic and chilli for 30 seconds. Add the coriander, cumin, onion and black pepper. Continue to stir-fry for 3–4 minutes.

❸ Add the turkey chunks, and stir-fry for about 3 minutes.

❹ Add the tomato paste, chopped tomatoes, coriander, sugar, ground almonds and tortilla chips. Stir-fry for a further 8–10 minutes, adding a little water if it becomes too dry.

❺ Stir in the chocolate until it has thoroughly melted and blended in.

❻ Check that the turkey is cooked right through by cutting a piece in half. It should be white all the way through. If not, continue stir-frying until it is. Season with salt.

Mediterranean Stir-fries

Think of the Mediterranean and you'll probably think sun, sea and sand. Your next thoughts may well be of that Spanish holiday you've been promising yourself for so long. I can't help you there, but I can do the next best thing. With the recipes in the next few pages, you can recreate some of those sunny, bright Mediterranean dishes, quickly and easily, in your own kitchen. There are stir-fried garlic prawns from Majorca, the fabulous paella from Spain, a delightful meatball recipe from Greece, and sardines from Turkey. Then it's on to Sicily for a brilliant spicy risotto, and Napoleon's island of Corsica, for a French-inspired creamy mussels dish called Mouclade.

Turkish Sardines

Preparation and cooking time: 15 minutes.
Freezing: not recommended. Serves 2 as a starter.

In Turkish seaside towns, fresh sardines are readily available. They are also easy to find at the fish counter here, so be sure to get some and try this simple Turkish-style stir-fry as a starter or a snack. You may also want to try whitebait in this recipe: allow 125 g (4 oz) of fish per person. Serve with a green salad and chilled white wine.

4 whole sardines, each weighing
   at least 50 g (2 oz)
2 tablespoons olive oil
1 teaspoon chilli powder

3 or 4 tablespoons sunflower oil
sea salt and freshly ground black pepper
a little plain flour
lemon wedges, to serve

❶ Wash and dry the sardines. Brush them with olive oil.
❷ Mix the flour with the chilli powder. Dab the sardines in this flour mixture.
❸ Heat the sunflower oil in a large frying-pan. Put the sardines in, and fry for about 10 minutes, turning from time to time.
❹ Sprinkle with the salt and pepper. Serve hot with the lemon wedges.

Spanish Paella

Preparation time: 10 minutes + 15 minutes cooking.
Freezing: recommended. Serves 4.

There is probably nothing more evocative of Spanish cuisine than paella. Apparently derived from the Iranian pullao, the Spanish have made it their own and here I have modified it for quick-and-easy stir-frying. Feel free to omit some of the ingredients if you wish, but on no account leave out the saffron! Together with the turmeric, it gives paella its distinctive colouring and that unique paella flavour. The finished dish is a substantial meal in itself, delightful with a chilled dry rosé wine. Mixed seafood salad is available frozen or at the fresh fish counter.

125 g (4 oz) chicken breast stir-fry fillets
150 ml (¼ pint) chicken stock
25–30 strands of saffron
3 tablespoons sunflower oil
½ teaspoon turmeric
2–4 garlic cloves, chopped finely
2 or 3 spring onions, chopped
1 tablespoon chopped red pepper
1 tablespoon chopped green pepper
1 tablespoon chopped celery

100 ml (3½ fl oz) dry sherry
200 g (7 oz) mixed seafood salad
4–6 cooked mussels, in shell
4–6 large cooked king prawns, shell on
50 g (2 oz) chorizo, sliced and quartered
1 tablespoon sun-dried tomato paste
500 g (1 lb) cooked rice
50 g (2 oz) garden peas, thawed
salt

❶ Cut the chicken into 2 cm (¾-inch) cubes.
❷ Heat the chicken stock and saffron in a wok. Add the chicken and simmer for about 10 minutes, stirring periodically.
❸ Heat the oil in a large frying-pan. Add the turmeric, garlic, onions, red and green pepper and celery. Stir-fry for 3–4 minutes.

❹ Add the sherry, seafood salad, mussels, king prawns, chorizo and sun-dried tomato paste. Stir-fry for about 4 minutes.
❺ Add the rice and peas. Briskly but gently (taking care not to break up the grains of rice), stir-fry everything until it is hot. Add the chicken and stock, and stir in.
❻ Season with salt. Arrange everything attractively on a large platter and serve.

Majorcan Stir-fried Garlic Prawns

Preparation and cooking time: 10 minutes.
Freezing: recommended. Serves 4 as a starter.

You'll find this favourite dish of the Spanish is often cooked on the beach, and nowhere is it nicer than in Majorca. They call it 'Gambas a la Plancha', which means, 'prawns (cooked) on the hot plate'. It works equally well cooked in the wok and goes superbly with Rioja wine, salad and garlic bread. Note the essential large amount of garlic in the ingredients.

500 g (1 lb) small cooked, shelled prawns
3 tablespoons olive oil
½ teaspoon tumeric
6–8 garlic cloves, chopped finely

4–6 spring onions, chopped
1 tablespoon finely chopped red pepper
salt

❶ De-vein the prawns if necessary and rinse them.

❷ Heat the oil in a wok until it is quite hot. Add the turmeric and garlic. Stir-fry for about 30 seconds. Add the onions and red pepper and stir-fry for 2 or 3 minutes more.

❸ Add the prawns and simply stir-fry them briskly until they are hot right through. Season with salt and serve.

Mussel Mouclade

Preparation and cooking time: 10 minutes.
Freezing: recommended. Serves 4 as a starter.

They say Napoleon loved this creamy, garlicky French mussel dish as much as he loved his island of Corsica. It is wonderful, especially when served with fresh crusty baguettes, straight from the bakery counter, to mop up the sauce. Note the oaky Chardonnay used in the cooking; why not drink the remainder of the bottle, well chilled, with the mussels?

2 tablespoons olive oil
2 tablespoons butter
½ teaspoon fennel seed
½ teaspoon celery seed
3 or 4 garlic cloves, sliced

1 kg (2 lb) cooked mussels in shell
125 ml (4 fl oz) white wine (e.g. Chardonnay)
142 ml (5 fl oz) double cream
1 tablespoon chopped fresh parsley
salt and freshly ground black pepper

❶ Heat the oil and butter in a wok until it is quite hot. Add the fennel and celery seeds and garlic. Stir-fry for about 30 seconds. Add the mussels and stir-fry for 2 or 3 minutes more.

❷ Add the wine and cream. When it simmers, add the parsley, and season with salt and pepper. Serve piping hot in bowls.

Sicilian Risotto

Preparation time: 10 minutes + 30 minutes cooking.
Freezing: recommended. Serves 4.

Sicily is the largest island in the Mediterranean, with a long history which even predates the Greeks and Romans, who began its traditions of wine production and wonderful food. This risotto is a meal in itself. Serve with chilled Sicilian Vernaccia white or rosé wines, or a red Chianti from Tuscany.

300 g (10 oz) risotto rice

50 g (2 oz) feta cheese in oil

1 tablespoon extra-virgin olive oil

25 g (1 oz) butter

2 teaspoons minced garlic

4 tablespoons dried onion flakes

8–10 large green olives, chopped

125 g (4 oz) peeled prawns in brine

3 or 4 bay leaves

1 tablespoon chopped sun-dried tomatoes in oil

2 teaspoons tomato purée

1 fresh green chilli, de-seeded and chopped
  finely (optional)

1 tablespoon chopped red pepper

2 teaspoons green pesto sauce

450 ml (¾ pint) thin clear vegetable stock

125 ml (4 fl oz) dry white wine

1 tablespoon chopped fresh oregano

1 tablespoon chopped fresh parsley

salt and freshly ground black pepper

To garnish:

about 4 tablespoons grated parmesan cheese

whole fresh oregano leaves

a few sprigs of parsley

❶ Immerse the rice in cold water, then rinse and drain it.

❷ Chop the cheese into small pieces.

❸ Heat the olive oil and butter plus 1 tablespoon of oil from the cheese in a large non-stick saucepan with a lid, and stir-fry the garlic for 30 seconds, then add the onion flakes, olives, prawns, bay leaves, sun-dried tomatoes, tomato purée, chilli (if using), red pepper, and pesto sauce. Stir-fry for about 5 minutes.

❹ Bring the stock to a simmer in its own pan.

❺ Add the rice to the stir-fry, and when sizzling, add a cupful of stock and the wine. Bring to a simmer, stirring, and then lower the heat, put the lid on, and stir now and again, until the stock is absorbed (about 3 minutes).

❻ Repeat this cupful by cupful with the remaining stock. Simmer on the lowest heat until all the stock is absorbed. Note that as the rice softens, the absorption time speeds up. Overall it will take about 10–12 minutes. Stir only to prevent it from sticking to the bottom of the pan.

❼ Add the oregano and parsley and season to taste. Fork everything together. Let the risotto stand in a warm place to rest for at least 10 minutes, and up to 30 minutes.

❽ Serve garnished with the oregano leaves, sprigs of parsley and some freshly grated parmesan.

Greek Meatballs

Preparation time: 15 minutes + 10 minutes cooking.
Freezing: recommended. Serves 2–4 as a starter.

These meatballs are guaranteed not to disintegrate. The key is to use the best quality steak your budget will allow. This recipe makes Greek kefte; add some spices and you have its close relative, India's kofta. Shape it round skewers, and you have seekh kebabs. Serve these meatballs with feta cheese and olive salad, a crunchy baguette, dripping with olive oil, and some strong Greek red wine.

375 g (12 oz) lean fillet steak
2 tablespoons dried onion flakes
2–4 garlic cloves, chopped
4–6 black olives, chopped
1 teaspoon dried oregano

3 tablespoons chopped fresh basil
½ teaspoon coarsely ground black pepper
½ teaspoon salt
3 or 4 tablespoons olive oil

❶ Chop the steak into smallish chunks.

❷ Put it, with all the other ingredients (except the oil), into the food processor in small batches (so as not to overload it) and pulse until it is quite smooth. You can do this in a mincer. Thoroughly mix everything together with your hands.

❸ Roll out the mixture into small balls, each about 2 cm (¾-inch) in diameter.

❹ Heat the oil in a large frying-pan. To prevent the balls from sticking together, add one ball at a time, turn it to seal it, and within seconds, add the next ball, and so on until all the balls are in (or until the pan is nearly full, in which case, you'll have to cook the meatballs in batches).

❺ Fry for about 10 minutes, carefully stirring and turning the balls, so that they are evenly cooked. Serve hot or cold.

European Stir-fries

My stir-fry voyage around the world would not be complete without a visit to our own backyard, Europe! My choice includes one recipe each from Austria, Germany, Hungary, France and Scandinavia. As for Britain, I've chosen a really unusual dish using wonderful British produce: asparagus, chestnuts, chicory and cream cheese.

British Asparagus and Chestnuts on Chicory Cheese

Preparation and cooking time: 15 minutes.
Freezing: not recommended. Serves 4 as a starter.

To represent Britain in our stir-fry collection here is a luxurious, spiced starter, good at any time of the year, but especially at Christmas.

16 asparagus spears
16 vacuum-packed or bottled chestnuts,
   halved
2 tablespoons sunflower oil
1 teaspoon celery seeds
1 garlic clove, chopped finely
2 or 3 spring onions, chopped finely
1 teaspoon finely chopped ginger (optional)
½ teaspoon garam masala (optional)
½ teaspoon chilli powder (optional)
salt
16 chicory leaves
75 g (3 oz) cream cheese
paprika

❶ Trim the asparagus just above the point where the stems are pithy. Microwave or steam the asparagus to tenderness.

❷ Heat the oil in a wok until it is quite hot. Add the celery seeds and garlic and stir-fry for about 30 seconds. Add the onions, ginger, garam masala, and chilli, if using, and continue to stir-fry for about 2 or 3 minutes more.

❸ Turn off the heat. Gently stir in the asparagus tips and the chestnuts. Season with salt. Allow to cool.

❹ Spread some cream cheese on to each chicory leaf. Top with the asparagus and chestnut mixture. Refrigerate and serve dusted with paprika.

Chicken Goulash

Preparation time: 10 minutes + 15 minutes cooking.
Freezing: recommended. Serves 4.

This is Hungary's national dish, modified to become an easy chicken stir-fry.

750 g (1½ lb) chicken breast stir-fry fillets

2 tablespoons vegetable oil

½ teaspoon celery seeds

½ teaspoon fennel seeds

1 teaspoon black peppercorns

2 or 3 bay leaves

2 teaspoons minced garlic

1 fresh hot red Hungarian paprika pepper or 1 Dutch red chilli, de-seeded and chopped finely

4 teaspoons paprika

4–6 spring onions, chopped

2 tablespoons finely chopped celery

2 tablespoons finely chopped fennel

400 g can of chopped Italian plum tomatoes

142 ml (5 fl oz) soured cream

salt

parsley sprigs, to garnish

❶ Cut the chicken into 2 cm (¾-inch) cubes.

❷ Heat the oil in a wok. Stir-fry the celery and fennel seeds, peppercorns, bay leaves, garlic, fresh paprika or chilli, and ground paprika, for a minute. To preserve the red colour, add 4 tablespoons of water and continue to stir-fry for a further minute.

❸ Add the chicken, onions, celery and fennel. Continue to stir-fry for about 3 minutes. It should sizzle, not burn. Add water again, if needed.

❹ Add the tomatoes with their liquid, and stir-fry for about 8 minutes.

❺ Check that the chicken is cooked by cutting a piece in half. It should be white all the way through. If not, continue stir-frying until it is.

❻ Add the soured cream and when hot, season with salt. Garnish with parsley sprigs.

French Lyonnaise Potatoes

Preparation time: 20 minutes + 20 minutes cooking.
Freezing: not recommended. Serves 4.

I've used leeks in this recipe instead of onion to give more colour to this classic French masterpiece. Serve this dish as an accompaniment, as a starter or as a snack. Its natural partner is that other masterpiece from Lyons, Beaujolais.

500 g (1 lb) potatoes

3 tablespoons butter

2 leeks, chopped

2 tablespoons finely chopped parsley

a few splashes of white wine vinegar

some snipped chives, to garnish

salt and freshly ground black pepper

❶ Parboil the potatoes (i.e. boil or steam until three-quarters cooked). Allow them to cool and slice them.

❷ Heat the butter in a wok. Stir-fry the leeks for about 5 minutes.

❸ Add the potato slices and stir-fry for about 5–10 minutes until they become golden, turning as necessary.

❹ Add the parsley and the vinegar. Stir-fry for a final minute. Season to taste and garnish with some freshly ground black pepper and chives.

Austrian Ceps Duxelle

Preparation and cooking time: 15 minutes.
Freezing: recommended. Serves 4 as a starter.

Ceps are one of several unusual mushroom varieties now more widely available. However, if you can't find ceps, use oyster mushrooms, field mushrooms or some other sort. Eat with hot buttered brown toast or cold as a sandwich or vol-au-vent filling.

375 g (12 oz) ceps or mushrooms

2 tablespoons walnut oil

1 tablespoon butter

2 or 3 garlic cloves, sliced

3 or 4 spring onions, chopped

1 green chilli, de-seeded and chopped finely
   (optional)

2 teaspoons paprika

6 black olives, quartered

60 ml (2 fl oz) red wine

90 ml (3 fl oz) double cream

salt and freshly ground black pepper

To garnish:

chopped parsley

snipped chives

❶ Chop the ceps or mushrooms into small cubes.

❷ Heat the oil and butter in a wok until it is quite hot. Add the garlic and stir-fry for about 30 seconds. Add the onions, chilli, paprika and olives. Stir-fry for 2 or 3 minutes more.

❸ Add the ceps (or mushrooms) and when they are sizzling, add the wine.

❹ Bring to a simmer and add the cream. Simmer for about 2 more minutes, stirring frequently until it is thick and creamy. Season to taste. Garnish with parsley, chives and freshly ground black pepper.

German Ham and Sauerkraut

Preparation and cooking time: 20 minutes.
Freezing: recommended. Serves 4.

Serve with buttered potatoes, Dijon mustard and a chilled schnapps or three!

300 g (10 oz) lean ham, cooked on the bone
2 tablespoons vegetable oil
½ teaspoon celery seeds
½ teaspoon fennel seeds
1–2 teaspoons green peppercorns in brine
2 or 3 bay leaves
2 garlic cloves, chopped finely

1 fresh red paprika pepper, chopped or 1
    tablespoon red bell pepper, chopped
125 g (4 oz) onion, chopped
3 tablespoons chopped celery
500 g (1 lb) sauerkraut
salt

❶ Chop the ham into 1 cm (½-inch) square cubes.

❷ Heat the oil in a wok. Stir-fry the celery and fennel seeds, peppercorns, bay leaves, garlic, and paprika or pepper for a couple of minutes. Add the onion and celery. Continue to stir-fry for 3–4 minutes.

❸ Add the ham and sauerkraut with its liquid. Stir-fry for about 5 minutes until hot. Season with salt and serve.

Scandinavian Stir-fry Pickled Herring and Prawns

Preparation and cooking time: 10 minutes.
Freezing: recommended. Serves 4 as a starter.

For many years, I used to visit all five Scandinavian countries, and more than once I came across 'Jannson's Temptation'. I don't know who Jannson is or was, or why the dish is called this, but here is my version. Serve hot or cold with salad and fresh rye bread, along with some chilled aquavit or schnapps.

2 tablespoons vegetable oil
4 marinated herring fillets
100 g (3½ oz) peeled prawns in brine
2 or 3 anchovies in oil, chopped
8 canned baby potatoes, sliced

1 firm eating apple, sliced
2 or 3 gherkins, sliced
150 ml (¼ pint) crème fraîche
sugar, to taste
salt

❶ Strain the herring fillets, reserving the onions and the liquid. Cut into bite-size pieces, discarding the skin, if you wish. Drain the brine from the prawns.

❷ Heat the oil in a wok. Add the herring, 3 or 4 tablespoons of its liquid, the prawns, anchovies, potatoes, apple slices and gherkins. Briskly stir-fry until it sizzles for a couple of minutes, ensuring that everything is hot all the way through.

❸ Remove the wok from the heat. Mix in the crème fraîche, and if you feel it needs it, add sugar and salt to taste.